The Locofo Anti-Trump Anthology:

Poems For Freedom

William Allegrezza, Editor

Locofo Chaps is an imprint of Moria Books dedicated to politically oriented poetry.

copyright © 2025
ISBN: 979-8-9869421-4-8

Locofo Chaps
9748 Redbud Rd
Munster, IN 46321

For inquiries, please email editor@moriapoetry.com.

Acknowledgements:
Some of these poems originally appeared in the following publications:

Alex Gildzen's "After the March" first appeared in his book <u>Still Marching</u> (River Dog 2021).

Carol Dorf's "No Twilight" was first published in *Unlikely Storeis*.

Carol Dorf's "When I pronounce the word future" was first published in *Wordpeace*.

Andrew K. Peterson's poems first appeared in *Ongoing Resuscitation (Indolent Books)* and *Blazing Stadium*

Mark Young's poems are taken from *The Complete Post Person Poems*, published by Sandy Press.

Table of Contents

Poems

Eileen R. Tabios

A Found Poetics

The world is a pond
of still water
When you throw
a pebble in it
the water ripples outward
from the stone's penetration
But the sole change
occurred with the arm that rose
The world settles back
into stagnant water
The world is a pond
of stagnant water

But we must still
throw the stones
Otherwise, we are not human
but corporations

Martha Deed

He's Baaaaa-a-a-a-ck

and you are a poet and a news nut
and one or the other
can take you down
to the bottom
of a toxic sea
and plus
you are so old
you may not live
to see the end of this

Now what?
Retreat is unappealing
Turning off the TV?
You lack the Will for that

Think
outside the box
an unfortunate construction
reminder of the coffin
our Democracy lies in

I swear upon the beat-up bible
I was awarded in the segregated South

Orange was never my favorite color

Do not give up your poetry
even if the darkest critic
would like to hang you
for writing them

10

Andrew K. Peterson

To the National Anthem

chrissi comped us bleacher seats
for singing you the night
the day game washed out
a baltimore twin bill
she got bumped for a chorus
of construction workers who
built the new monster section
spent the rainout
getting shitfaced at the cask

their rendition resembled
the welding of the lugnuts
not so much scott key
they gave it their all
as any kirkwood buttressing luxury
at the aging lurch of chaseball

the troops had just entered afghanistan

the last row bros
unfurled a great flag
to show who they were for
smoke behind
get tossed out from
for fighting some
other last row bros

me? i'm just keeping score
waiting for another spaceman

11

to play earth opera
for his jaunt in from the pen
when the game's well out of hand

in the end, what is there?
to talk of passing time
the weather is strange
no summer this year
in the days of the war
but the red sox are winning

anyway, we stood
against you
out of habit and duress
in the humid blaze of stars and stars and stars and stars
and stars and stars and stars and stars and stars and stars
and stars and stars and stars and stars and stars and stars
and stars and stars and stars and stars and stars and stars
and stars and stars and stars and stars and stars and stars
and stars and stars and stars and stars and stars and stars
and stars and stars and stars and stars and stars and stars
and stars and stars and stars and stars and stars and stars
and stars and stars and stars and stars
forever

Holly Crawford

You're Going to Love This

loosely and softly roll around
buy, we don't buy
stretch it out
take it
add a pinch
push it in then out
love their tradition
force the fruit
push it down
drill baby drill
more force
smooth it off
  use your hands
they just let you do it
your whole hand
now the rolling pin
real power
more, you can play
but no soggy bottoms
well done

Carol Dorf

No, Twilight, and the Law

I tell my child
No, twilight is a given
I can't slow the day's passage to night

In the photo of the boardwalk through the swamp
I support my child
as they lean back to look up at the trees
in a inversion of flight

For a while we called
it the Rumplestilskin phase
toddler jumping up and down in fury
Luckily the old oak floor held solid

There are so many things
about the world I would change for you if I could
though I wouldn't do anything about the dogs
in costumes participating in the Pride Parade

And then – You travelled to the pride parade
wearing wings – with friends who also found
wings to celebrate, and now you are all flown

All these laws that are disrupting
your flight path – Not in my backyard
but I'll do my best

Anthony Salazar

Our Retribution

You want the felon
because crime is high

      and yet I see communities webbing hands against
      the men of unveiled hoods

      the othered lurking in the shadows of your
      surveilled borough yearning for a deaf ear to hear

      the unjustified scapegoated by your own fear of
      irrelevance

You want the rapist
because women need a protector

      and yet I see agonizing miscarriages screaming in
      lots from docs afraid of murmured heartbeats

      bleeding bonnets placed on the heads of offreds
      oblivious to the horrors of tomorrow

      a vote of infidelity when unaccompanied by a man
      who surely knows all too well what lies within the
      horizon

You want the racist
because borders are open

      and yet I see gleaming eyes of the suffered

15

cautiously cocooned by the promise of america

dying towns reinvigorated by the tired, the poor,
the huddled masses yearning to breathe free the
wretched refuse of your teeming shore

concealed workers beaten by a hard day's work
whispering to their young mija todo estará bien

You want the strongman
because the kgb needs a tough man

and yet I see a coward drowning in the lago of
big mac sauce and desperation

eager to unchain the cuffs
of daniels' vengeance

But I also see hope of tomorrow
a time where a madam doesn't sound so scary

I see the truth unraveling to set us free
from the tyranny of echoing promises
souring from the garbage of tomorrow's yesterday

I see my flag regaining glory
to the republic for which it thirsts

one nation indivisible by the invisible

and justice for all

Mark Cunningham

A FINE DAY
no vacseen

FEAR ITSELF
di~~his~~hercence

DIE!VERSITY
a bad idei

MAXIM
we must snatch every opportunity
and every snatch is an opportunity

SEE IF THE RUBES WILL BUY IT
demo cracy

Rachael Ikins

A Leap of Faith

Jump, he says, it's gonna hurt a little.
You climb the rungs of the bridge railing.
Wind nips your ears; your hands slip on coated ice.
Jump! he says, I love you, you look down at streaming
traffic,
shuffle your feet,

jump.

Smash onto a van's windshield, mom taking three kids to
        school.
Slews across six lanes, slams into the bridge abutment.
Like an accordion, five vehicles cram into hers. A Prius
        driven
by a nurse coming home from the late shift ER,
white Ford pick-up loaded with bags of mulch,
a bus full of Sunday school campers. Bodies thrown
around inside like fish in a tank. A dump truck smacks
a hundred-year-old tree.

Branches drag power lines hissing to asphalt.
People scream. Crumpled Chevy leaks, gas ignites.

For three weeks newscasters will say residents heard
the explosion 4 miles away.
For three weeks pundits will say
someone should do something

about suicides off that bridge.

Who? the Santa Ana whistles, sparks
through dry grasses, road shoulder. They flutter like
butterflies over a retaining wall. Neighborhood asleep.
Shingles, plastic play sets burst into unholy life.
Fire gobbles everything it sinks its claws into.
Exhales black smoke.
Don't inhale.

EMTs wearing masks pull you off crumpled hood
desperate to jam an IV where your faded Nazi tattoo
bleeds into skin.
****
Thoughts and prayers, your funeral,
someone shouts, "He died a patriot!"

As if suicide off a bridge into traffic which,
like a snake shedding skin leaves serial death behind,
all because someone wearing thick orange pancake
makeup spouted stories too good to be true as he passed
you a red solo cup at a rally, of something that tasted
bloody,
but he said he loved you so you quaffed it,
is something to be proud of.

Other victims' families sue yours and fire fighters
from three countries still battle the blaze weeks later
that began with
your leap of faith

Joel Chace

What Rough Beast

Against which, entrance the war, and
 its peddlers, who cherish desolation's beauty,
with its wells of ever-wakeful grief,
letting that low music in, giving
it ear and resonance. *If only*
it were not so green; we
should like to make the grass
deathly pale. Against them all, hold
 up Santa Lucia's eyes so that
those mongers go blind and turn
into crows that see only faithlessness
            enter their graves.

Sheri Reda

Caudal Autonomy and the Lizard Brain

How can we forget? Dragons do roam the landscape
strafed by scabs and livid scars
produced by the relentless sweep of their tails. Their
      marauds
shudder your troubled sleep in the shade of their
      mansions and Japanese maples.
Dragons teach no such thing as enough: more
than us they want honor, integrity, courage, kindness, love
for dragons and their boundless need and
fairness doesn't come into it. We'll have to give what
      we can't spare
again. Kiss and tuck them in
again. They will never be sated. They'll have your tail
and more if you can't detach,
but what they want is to be dead without dying.

Jared Schickling

After the Election but before the Orange Menace

I see something beneath my skin,
a pulse at the throat of my being,
a sharpness—silent, small,
and secret beneath the thickening sky.
Once, I was a fire that ate my own tail.
Now, I am the moon's face,
blinking against the slow sand,
every grain a light falling from my hand, o

breathe in—what is that?
A city of rust. A woman,
her lips stitched with brittle thread.
I touch her with no hands,
only the shadow of my legs bending,
footfalls, then I am lost—
the breath of the air here so thin it grows teeth.
I could swallow myself in it,
but who would see? Who would ever know
the color of the water I drink
or the pulse of the dust as I step?
She tells me the world is a lie
and has forgotten which way it bends.
I know only the heat of an air
that boils my bones,
that says: "If you are nothing,
we are everything."
This is the story, the story
I will tell to the mirrors and to the dogs.

There will be nothing left of it now.

The earth smiles in a laugh that doesn't echo.
That's all. Nothing more to say.
There are no stars left. No roads.
Only the feeling of the wind on the back of my neck,
a kind of hot sin I can't speak.
I am the hand and the horizon.
I am lost, and I am found,
but always, always
the same.

Jill Stockinger

The Grand Ole Party

The furniture
is being rearranged,
the music is hypnotic,
and all kinds of games
are being played
while the country
is sinking
into the gas-filled swamp.

Angel Altamirano

Wednesday Morning

Tired eyes brace at morning light
Then at screen light.
First sight tense pupils absorb is
A man who deems my family "vermin"

Won.

I could have basked in honeyed ignorance
Just a moment longer.
Before rooting around for news
That makes me forget how to breathe.

Anyway, I have to go to work.
  At times I can almost steady myself.
A shield of gold is all I have for my family.
  Yet my bones shake, they will for a long time.

Mom calls.
Cheer almost cloaks her terror. I do the same.
Til her voice cracks.
She shoves it down again, way down, with chatter.

"Weather's getting cold!"
"How's work?"
"How's your dog?"
And at the end,

"You should call a lawyer."
"Yeah."

Likely in vain against what's coming.
Better than nothing.

Petitions lay unseen. For decades.

So that. Years from now. A stranger

Can at last stamp my family.

"Not Vermin".

Come January I always check the news
To know how laws are changing, how to brace for it.
And every morning
Is a Wednesday morning.

Martha Deed

RED COVID

I have Great Assets. Plus I Won.
I wish RED COVID on them all.
Witch Hunters robbed me of my throne.
I have Great Assets. Plus I Won.
Failed FAKE NEWS MEDIA is done.
My Militia Base will kill them all.
I have Great Assets. PS I Won.
I wish RED COVID on them all.

Pledge of Allegiance

I OWE NO ALLEGIANCE TO THIS RAPIST KING
Nor to the billionaire lackeys fawning his power grab
Nor lawyers afraid of prosecuting this American traitor
whose intimates are dictators, whose deals are self- interest
26 women claim sexual assault -I owe them credence
Government papers stored at Mar-a-Lago illegally.
How many lawyers stack our Supreme Court? All of them!
Liars and deniers of Global Climate Change vs Frackers
       &Miners
Is this Mass Hypnotism/Delusion/Hallucination -all RED
CAPS?
How come Barabbas wins again? You who love dictators-
       GO LIVE THERE!
Hotels in Moscow , Gaza ,Lebanon, Yemen, Syria-none
       bear the RUMP logo
Because you can fool the people all the time, but
       Cassandra sees -
THE SKY IS FALLING! Apocalypse and Armageddon just
       shook hands(again)-
And, by the way-YOU'RE FIRED!

Thérèse Bachand

FASCIST PHONETICS

ch

cherish the child

and the chick that

bred the chap

and the chair

he now sits on

chop

chop

finish the cheese

and chips

"childhood is the

most finite of ages"

the churlish daycare

worker chalked onto

asphalt w/angst

cr

crucial to not crash

cry

crown your sorrows

you cross yourself in the crucifix of

Crusaders

that crib is several centuries gone

I criss-cross the

paveways

détente with crows

fr

a frown from

a friend unhinged

as frost on a

field discourages

a frog's tempered

frolic

fugitives of fraternity =

freedom's fugue

pr

pretend to be   president

primping your

press

prying into   women's

nomenclatures

prettying

your tressed

prop

(probing our   protests)

presently, even

your print is   probably

praying for

you

          tw

you twasn't

then twilled

twittered

twatted

twitched in

twilight

amongst your

crochety

twiggy

twosome

wh

a wheel was whipped

by when

why?

what has happened to

when, where, who?

WHO - - - WHOO

WHO - - - WHOO

wondered the owl,

walled up behind

descending willow

Martha Deed

All Brokey

Il y a quelque chose qui ne va pas
(all brokey) the two-year-old announced
from her *chaise haute* one rainy morning
in Paris where the sun went behind
a cloud in June and in October
had not been seen again, the mist
of steam and rain dulling the red
roofs of Paris down the streets
to Notre Dame which hung like a cloud
above the Seine. As I bent to pick up
the remains of her blue plastic cup
off the white and black tile floor
that day, I did not have time to complain
as I have now. And now the complaints
do not involve household floors
but rather congressional floors
and not crumbs left on my desk
by the cracker-eating child
but the crumbs of justice left
on the Resolute desk in the Oval
Office for us to save and I am not
prone to optimism which is a shame
because even in Paris – a far cry
from DC – optimism – though
a figment of a fertile imagination
would be a help because now it is not
Covid that has rendered French cuisine
dust in my mouth but the news from home
where no one objects to my American

accent but where it is very hard
to sit still for the goings-on
and even harder to sleep

Oregon Blue
bluer than cobalt blue
appearing now
but not a sign
neither deliverance
nor harbinger of woe
in this development

of a pigment
hitherto unknown
Oregon Blue

when all the sky is gray
will be something to show
to the children
& say

this was once ours

"encyclopedia of skin infections"

after the upside down crucifixions
& the outcry, there were calls to moderate tone

i know those people

"bible verse checkpoints"

maps shred · in the gamefied martyrdom
tired of pretending · torched bookshelves

passing the buck · abort causality
only ammo · knows the way home

harry k stammer

turn table 43,4
[ringing bells] DC g u t d
rip r d paper DC [ringing bells]
alarms t constant "non" blown smoke up
[ringing bells] DC "non" tion our ask

Janine Harrison

Doc, Dopey, Grumpy...Rice!

"St. Paul's congregation --
come wash your hands!"
Three-fourths of the room rise
from backless benches.
"No less than 20 seconds!"
We three, in the last one-quarter
enter after, the sink-lined hallway
everything symmetrical, sterile.

Birthed into the warehouse next --
"Eight to a station!"
We stand with five nearby.
"Listen carefully to the directions!
Don't do anything until I'm done!"
We with advanced degrees
returned to high school
a prison work program
don our active listening ears:
Vitamins
Vegetables
Soy
Rice
Bag
Weigh
Seal
Box
Repeat.

Mother of a middle schooler

of a grade schooler
assigns places
at our metal island
in the din
within white walls
beneath beams.
We begin:
The nine year old
has two ladles
no knowledge of "level"
I woman the soy

Mark the rice
Lynne the bags
and a one, two
and a three, four
and a
one two three four...
girl getting better.
Our first box
of 16 bags:
A collective
"Woo-hoo!"
Musical positions.
The tweenager spills vitamins
What a waste. No waste!
but mentally snaps back
to scoop duty after.
Second box:
"Hey, hey, ho, ho,
hun-ger has got to go!"
Energy heats up
from simmer.

Do they have this in Haiti?
With no mail service,
do children receive
this daily nourishment?
The boy in filthy underwear
belly an empty bowl
who followed me
down a dirt road...

Girl takes the rice scoop,
Lynne ambi-ladles
vitamins and veges
I still scoop soy.
We are mothers.
"Lions,
Tigers,"
"and bears,"
"and rice!" Giggles the girl.

"Donner,
Dasher,"
"Blitzen,"
"Rudolph!"
We "Yay!"

"Snow White,
Rapunzel,"
"Belle,"
"Cinderella!"
We smile wide.

"Ten minutes left!"

We double time.

"Uno,
Dos!"
"Tres!"
"And rice!"
We laugh.

We laugh
till the last bag
is sealed and stored,
till our surfaces
are scoured,
till we are dismissed
to wash and sit.

A vivid sign
hangs over our station:
"Dominican Republic."
I mad dash past
other stations:
"Sudan," I see,
"India"
"Afghanistan"
"Ukraine"
"Honduras."
People are exiting.
As I turn to go,
I spy it:
"Haiti."
Shoulders sigh...

We sit silent

after our two-hour
power stint.

"Thanks to your work
tonight,
145 children
across the globe,
will eat everyday
for a year!"

Best Saturday night
ever spent.

Diana Magallón

Tryanilarias

How long, tyrant, will you abuse our patience? How long will your hate algorithms continue to divide society? Where will your arrogance that builds walls in a globalized world lead? How can you not be moved by the outcry of those who, fleeing war and poverty, seek refuge in this land of opportunities that you have turned into a fortress? Do you not feel that your policies are now fully exposed and that your cruelty is now recognized and, as it were, taken in hand by the keen knowledge and judgment of all these people? Which of us do you think is unaware of what you did when you expelled those who, with their labor, have contributed to your wealth? How long will we continue to endure a leader who hates those who make him great?

Oh, the times! Oh, the borders!

Melinda Luisa de Jesús

Hubris

It's almost as if you know they're
not
really yours

The way you keep
demanding your
ownership of
asserting your
dominion over
the land
the water
women's bodies
the will of the people.
What will you claim next—the air?

Just know
The gods are watching...

Stake of the Union

Missed your tea in China
Grab 'em by the puzzlements
Grab 'em by the puns
Law is a state of consciousness

Scrap democracy for the minors
Set accurate history on fire
ignited by lies
Politics as policies of vengeance
Rallies as statements of law

Put a T in China
Put taxes on an American alphabet
Make America Great Again merch
made in China
Pawn the banned books of USA in China
Convert it all into Bibles
Sell what's bought from China in China
Convert it all into guns
Move the East coast and West coast to China
Use the cash for bribes and fines

In the White House but still wants
to pickpocket islands and territories
Buy the new principles
of American democracy in China
Put the blame on China
Find a scapegoat in China
Find a doppelganger in China

About two and a half billion acres of land—
that's USA to take pity on
The one and a half billion people in China
might be able to pitch in
and buy a solid acre or two each
There's not more to it
Made in China

Europe watching a four-year
mockumentary of a country
Press play
it's high tech
and live
Hostile Tesla
Hostile formerly known as Twitter
Hostile social medias of Meta
The White House the wedding dress
of the States left at the altar
And he grabs 'em by the pussy

Tyranny comes with a prize
Democracy comes with a prize
The escalating insanity
sprung from an attempted
hostile takeover
as the tip of an iceberg
At what point
does a Western country
void that very definition?
The United States of Two Societies
Living as One Country
Freedom always for sale
at second hand value
The United States of Bullshit and Breakthrough

Eileen R. Tabios

The Obsolescence of Star Maps

From "The Monobons of Nuance"

The world began to end when the President of the United States informed the world that stars were missing from star maps. Havoc began to reign in ways as numerous as the religions forsaken by humanity. Too many people behaved predictably: many killed others simply from the inevitability of being killed—that they committed murder instead of suicide proved to the Powerful Ones that their decision was justified. You see, any species that used celestial bodies as fuel was intelligent enough to discern who didn't warrant their existence—like those strangling the same planet that allowed them to survive and whose lack of nuance proved the reductivity of their slogan "Kill or be killed." To such a combination of ingratitude, venality and stupidity, the Powerful Ones released a spare star. They held back the radiation from the small room where I typed on my laptop so that I could finish this report for their files. Beyond the window, steel skyscrapers kept imploding into grey powder. Then I arrived at my last words whose utterance is fittingly an exercise in futility:

it sucks to be the last eyewitness to Earth

Andrew K. Peterson

To Capital

for Patti Smith

To my fine trembling fits of button-down blue work spirit gone
numb as fingers
flogged buffaloes gallop backward toward the overdue do-overs of
the infinite...

Lemon-nimble
in a late epoch of wildflowers
reflective but forgetful
stardust sodium fades
the serpentine divine
hisses counter-spells
chloroform's acid flood
closed vowels locked in achromatic
spewed from disintegrating front-liners
dipped in masks of androgynous mist
smoldering gold
ripped from bones used to re-bud the capitol dome
rasping through second winter
the rot and woof encroachment
on morning's arhythmic field

I go yellow in the locker room
when they tease me in my Tommy shirt
when they're caught on camera
dealing Boris Karloff dreams
to blue hunters in full harvest
when payday unspools
lemon-nimble, lovelorn,

when my hopeful one scrapes
lines of ash from the trillion-dollar bill
to burn anew
a new American standard
O tiger eyelets leering forth
from rapture's halved pyramids
return me to the longing pulse
sucked from oak-knotted muscles
as I stoop in a capitalist gangster lean
with the ache they mean to bend me away from you with

See Me Feel Me
Touch Me Heal Me

O fashion me a jacket
out of grief –
a false protection
from false & tactless crumbles
of faraway star death
as green-eyed dyes swirl away
ghosted from my fingerprints
unbuttoning this decadent redemption
from within this bottomless
                    buttonless
                        blue

Thom Woodruff

CALM @THE CENTER

TRANQUIL IN THE WATERS
When sleep comes-deeply dreaming
When wakefulness arrives-eyes, opening.
Between storms, moments deepen ,extending
Architecture of Emotions -a whistle of Golden Leaves
Rustle in this Deep Forest....Stillness in motion.
Silence Illuminates-Songs Extend us...Harmonies are
        Haven
I hear more than i see...Feel more than i know.
9 billion leaves on our One World Tree
And it's Fall/ing.

Frank Johnson

The Day Democracy Died

On the Fifth of November 2024
the US elected Trump once more,
a cult-hero charlatan and conman who
says truth is lies and lies are true,
has been declared a sexual predator,
would dearly love to be a dictator,
is racist, sexist, fascistic, bombastic,
avaricious, crooked and narcissistic,
sucks up to bullies like Vladimir Putin
but bullies anyone who's weaker than him,
is the sociopath boss of a mafia clan,
convinces the gullible that he's their man,
whose guiding principle is divide and rule,
who incited the mob to attack the Capitol
during which six died and many were injured,
is the only president twice impeached,
is soft on White Supremacists,
only rates people of high net worth,
whose rule will be ruinous for life on Earth,
who favours mephistophelians like Elon Musk,
demeans diplomacy and undermines trust,
calls himself a genius but talks like a twit,
is the first former president to be convicted,
was facing a slew of serious court cases,
is Christ come again for the Christian Alt-Right
(how oxymoronic!), whose Truth Social website
is nonsense and lies, who sends thoughts and prayers
after every mass shooting but won't ever dare
get rid of the guns, is the economy's saviour

with a brilliant record of business failure,
who mishandled Covid calamitously,
is a slob and a creep, is all Me-Maga-Me
and nothing else matters,
and for the sake of whose pride
the 5th of November in the USA
was the day that democracy died.

Geneva Chao

A Poem for the Most Important Man in the World

Los Angeles, 10 January 2025

Dear Donnie,
I get it now. For the longest time
why anyone with as many golf courses and casinos
as you would want to ride around in Air Force One
being in charge of all the fractured dreams and
        resentments
that are America escaped me. Why not just bask,
I thought, what any normal person would do,
shut your eyes and turn up the music.
But that's not you. You're a different type
of guy. Bigger. You need more.
Not just your voice in every speaker
and your face on every screen,
but to matter. I get it. It's human nature
to want to matter and if the only way we can do it
is by flicking a lighter at a sleeping person
and watching them burn, or kicking a paraplegic
when they're down, or grabbing them
by the pussy, or bankrolling a foreign war,
that's what we do.
You need attention.
My grandfather used to swallow a bottle
of pills and go sit out on his front stoop
so they could pick him up, pump his stomach.
He just wanted someone
to take notice. Maybe your way

is better. My grandmother waited
until he went two towns over,
to buy her favorite strawberries,
and shot herself in the face.
Your way is definitely better.
No one's gonna stop you
in your tracks, crestfallen,
the strawberries scattering on the ground.
No one's gonna catch you sleeping.
Your voice is in all our ears,
all the time, currently jeering at the governor
as if the farmers' ire about almonds
had caused epic drought and winds.
Maybe it does. Everything is connected,
after all, and we don't have the attention
span to notice. The city
is burning. The world is burning,
and all we can see is you,
orange-gold and ubiquitous,
like the Taco Bell in the movie
where everything is a Taco Bell.
You're good at what you do.
Most of us care a little too much,
invest energy in futile things, like gardens,
or libraries, or poems, or paraplegics,
or children who might not make it anyway,
or who might grow into something we dislike,
or buildings and bridges
that might go up in flames tomorrow. Many of us
will be found with that garden hose
still clutched in our hand,
ashen and silent in rubble. And for what?
Nobody hears that last wish we send out,

however much we loved
what we failed to save. But you,
you aren't trying to save
anything, which is why you're winning.
I get it. You're great
at what you do. The best.
Fantastic. Your cadence
is in all our mouths,
maybe even forming those worthless
wishes. We can't help ourselves.
We who can't stop loving each other
or that child who might not make it,
or who might turn out to be someone
else who doesn't metabolize love.
We're fettered with the garden hose
and the pool pump and the cat carrier
and the frantic chickens and the wounded
cougar, a bunch of attachments
trailing behind us,
getting stuck on things.
Eventually we'll stop moving.
The wind howls, and
you're still talking
about how the burning homes and hearts
and all that love and history turned
to bits of grey and white on the wind
is our own fault,
and we're still sweeping up ash and praying
for rain, and weeping for the grief
of people we've never met and people
we used to know, wondering
if we'll make it out alive,
or at all, and if anyone will feel all

the beautiful wishes we're whispering
as we go about these humble
tasks, playing a kind of Russian Roulette
we all have too much stake in,
counting all the things we love
and can't live without, or
preparing to live without them,
if only we do make it out alive.
If only. That's the secret you know, isn't it?
Nobody leaves alive. But everyone gets
one call, calls out
to the most essential person,
the person whose voice they crave
when hope is gone.
And the human heart
is hungry. We all want to be
that most essential heart
to another heart, their prayer
as the plane goes down,
the wish they send up into the sky
as they smolder. I get you, Donnie.
You've got a big heart, that's obvious,
so hungry,
a big gaping maw of a heart
and you're never gonna be that guy
for anyone.
So this is how you get there,
be the one guy
a whole nation can praise or blame
but no one can look away from,
be the motorcycle accident
on the Interstate and
engulf all of us in your flames,

bless your heart.
Bless your hungry, hungry heart.

Holly Crawford

you can just do it
rapidly, affordable, trampling
down love , so big, biggest
 a diamond, unlikely
judges looking, when
nothing like it, ever
shush, you're not President
quickly, let's go
move, that's right folks
I want now, immediately
just do it
well, I think
It's the Gulf of the unlikely
I don't care, they
no opinions

Andrew K. Peterson

Work Song

after Gina Myers

"All rest my powers defy" – John Donne

Summer falls in false terminus: labor
abandons austere measure. Watch a film about sharks
and monoliths devouring an ocean tourist by tourist.
Work Songs we cover every day until effort's reassigned

or the feather rudders yesterday's Facetime in the park.
Cicada's hurdy-gurdy (my powers *deify*), but I didn't see a
dragonfly to lessen the decay or store my body's rest until
the sweat dries and the sea-carved salt from our backs
carries back to the reef what Rihanna knows:

repeat a word enough & its spiral collapses,
incomprehensible, a harvest at noisy dusk offering its
unspent labor to the sky. The height of my fight syndrome:
broken drinking glasses, dusted magnets falling behind
the fridge three tenements high.

To do the work so I can rest the rest & make it (better?
make good? or just: to make it). My worth is worth the
effort:

work work work work work
work work work work work
mmh mmh mmh mmh mmh
wah wah wah wah wah
ahhh wah wah wah wah wah waaah

A radiant hole, I fall
into, until I labor, &
I, in labor,
lie

PUBLIC RECLUSES

THEIR SPEECH SIGNIFICANT
Their silences profound
Greatest Distance? To the Core of their Soul
To be at ease with yourselves
(whoever they may be at the time..
Then to Greet The Unknown with a wry smile
Librarians, readers, classical music composers
Access this simple and arcane technique-
To inhabit each moment fully, without the need
for distractive enterprises. There will always be films,
and books ad infinitum. News repeats on a 24 hour cycle.
To take oneself out of the loop. To be at ease in silence.
Maybe meditation. Perhaps casual observations.
Looking within the world to better absorb and integrate.
Perhaps you have eggshell habits (easily annoyed by
        others)
Deep breathing and relaxation techniques.T hey all add to
        silence
Within and in every relationship-Make space to breathe
        alone
and together..

Whose Side Is God On?

In an attempt to keep his evangelical Christian voters,
	Donald
Trump says that Joe Biden winning the presidency would
	hurt God.
Do evangelical voters really believe that a 77-year-old guy
obviously past his physical prime could injure a being they
consider omniscient and omnipotent? What did Trump's
evangelical voters think of Trump's implying such divine
	weakness,
or when he had peaceful protesters across the street from
	the White House
teargassed and hit with batons so that Trump could stroll
	over and hold up
a bible upside-down in front of an historic church? Does
	God
approve of teargassing peaceful protesters or of a
	sociopathic
politician holding up a bible that wasn't even his own for a
	quick
publicity photo? As Trump argues for the risk of fraud
	when it comes
to mail-in voting, except in Florida where he knows he will
	need the mail-in
votes of Republican seniors, would God vote in person, if
	she
or he could, during a highly contagious pandemic? Advice
	columnist,
E. Jean Carroll, has just won a New York court case
	allowing her

to proceed with her civil suit against Trump for rape—do
      religious
Christians really believe that Jesus would approve of a
      candidate
accused by dozens of women of a range of sexual assaults
      from self-admitted
groping to rape? Everything I've read in the Old and New
      Testaments,
from the Golden Rule to Jesus's preaching of compassion
      and mercy, argues
against the malicious selfishness of Trumpian right-wing
      policies,
whether economic, ecological, or racist; or when it comes
      to his desire to build
a new generation of Earth-destructive nukes. As a
      longtime atheist, I believe
that I know what God would want better than most
      evangelicals, and it sure
as hell or no-hell isn't Trump.

Charles A. Perrone

Trumpostic

Treasonous
Rapacious
Unfit
Misogynic
Prevaricating

Treacherous
Ranting
Uncouth
Mendacious
Petty

Traitorous
Raving
Usurious
Misguided
Predatory

Thievish
Racist
Uncivilized
Misogynistic
Plunderous

Two-timing
Ridiculous
Untruthful
Megalomaniacal
Perfidious

Nico Vassilakis

The Next Stretch

Is quietly despondent

Is surrounded by indentation

Damn Chachalaca
Boom chimichurri

Who can Trump guilty on all counts

You know there's a timeline when
You know there's a timeline

The king is dead
Long live the king

Damn chimichurri
Boom Chachalaca

*

At the end of my vocabulary
I just stare and listen

I think it's morning now
Toward eleven or inside seven

Quandary distributed evenly

The teleprompter easing all pain

No more ruffled lapel

John Stickney

Forts

We won world wars
out of forts
Fort Benning
Fort This
Fort That
They changed the names
of the forts
We won two world wars
out of the forts

(found poem - Donald Trump quote, Jan. 20, 2021)

D. Reed Whittaker

Antifa .

In darkness deep, where truth cowers,
Fascism tightens its iron muzzle.
With rigid thought, and voices mute,
The cult of fear completes the puzzle.

The missing pieces are now in place.
Project 2025, the roadmap to control.
Rights are gone, freedom lost, the end?
Greed took it all, a country they stole.

No way to get it back, no way.
Corruption is everywhere, truth hides.
Evil rules the land, the cult won.
Good has gone? Where does honor abide?

While the battle's lost, not the fight.
'Twas first the Tories, then the slavers.
We won those fights; the war goes on.
It's now the MAGAtts, and billionaires.

While much is wrong with our country,
There is much which is right, and much good,
Our politics isn't one of them.
Stay in the fight, resist as we should.

They may dim the light, but only for a bit.
Resist the fascists, reclaim your country.
America, America,
Antifa, Antifa, Antifa.

Michael Helsem

every reason for silence

i am sick · of complicated redemptions
being sent to Siberia · in order to save my soul
i am sick of making meaning · materialize like ectoplasm
the psychotic break · of my feckless countrymen
  dismal to relate
turned into text responses · read by no one
  i am sick of these feelings
of dread for my loved ones · the lingering culture
  & from time to time for myself
that lucky bystander · & abysmal philosopher
caught in my own · complicated redemption

Jill Stockinger

Sing a Song of Government

"I Don't Care" and "Look Away"
Sit next to "No Opinion"
To Vote on Very Important Rules
To Govern Our Whole Nation.

The Committee Chair is "Gimme Some"
Who Rules with Iron Hand,
With Pay to Play and Kickbacks
The True Law of our Land.

Our Mantra is Lift Up the Rich
And Help ME Line my Pocket;
We Don't Care Who it Hurts–
Getting Money is the Object.

Break the Rules? All the Time
And then Exonerate
Whoever We Want and Proceed
To Tell Everyone it's GREAT!

The Poor will never Count
As we Grab More than we Need,
For Mammon is our Only God
And we Glory in our Greed!

Dawn Hanson Smart

The Collapse

The throne canted sideways
The dance and punching fists
Threatening to tip it off the dais
Crown slipping down over one check
Smudging the pancake makeup
Tainted imperial robes
Sluffing from his shoulders
Puddling around his feet
Sawed-off handcuffs
Dangling from one wrist
New picks crowding in
Seeking the means to buttress the structure
Or find the best photo op stance
But what's this? SpaceX to the rescue?
The throne wobbling from the pitched takeoff
Teetering, grasping armsrests, sliding
Hanger-oners clutching for a handhold
Everyone, holding their breaths

Nico Vassilakis

DOUBLE APOCALYPSE

This time it's worse
Than you ever thought
Revulsion is everywhere
Either side is a dead end
A double apocalypse

A tingling tangled numbness

This time it's the media
That wants to be president

Godzilla through and through
Yes to stealing
Yes to time and money

It's an infected conclusion, religious
delusion and outright fraud and theft

Nothing aligns with how you
Think about nothing now

Sheri Reda

Body Politic

Speak for yourself they still say
don't presume you know
what anybody else is thinking
but the same they doesn't call me
by my searching brown eyes or
leaping heart. The same they insists
on calling me American or bitch or dago
or Jew or white or what are you: Mexican? Indian? Paki?
Where are you from, exactly? I know the drill
but the fossil fuel of the past lies deeper.
Whoever you are, whoever I am to you,
I'm sorry for what's happened.
Overjoyed
we're both alive and still breathing the damaged air.
Happy to be you, which is to say, me.

Janine Harrison

The Hippies Had It Right (Almost)

*Based on Farm Community in Summertown, Tennessee,
America's longest running commune, which was begun in 1971,
transformed into an "intentional community" in 1983, and
thrives yet today.*

Good, good, good vibrations
led the commune to
land in Tennessee to
one house and two barns.
Where they grew through
recycled wood and tin,
where each established home
contained a village to
raise the children,
where each village
raised a garden:
Crisp, cool Kelly green cukes and
earthy kale.
Where they sowed soybeans
eaten on tortillas
made from flour, fat,
water, salt, sold to locals.
Where they wore
handsewn clothes, a
shoestring survival
based on trust and + energy,
where what you think,
what you do
matters.

They righted a school
where respecting
Mama Earth
sun power
equality
equity
of resources
across the globe
was taught,
where it was made plain:
"It is your responsibility to
make the world

a better place."
By the late 70's
these peace-lovers –
English major dropouts & like types –
morphed into organic farmers,
into "eco-minded entrepreneurs."
There were struggles.
Aren't there always issues
in first waves? Second?
Still:
Why didn't society
take cues from them
back then?
If we had,
where would we be
today?

Todd Stoll

he fiiled his veins with the vanity of virtual
sanity to deflect his affects from
genuflecting in the mirror of the eclipse

where solar lips burned the passing ships in
the far right of his sight set on endless
night

to sail in the wails of thunder as the wonder
of a dictator dictating strength as the length
of sights obscene

Politician

Like the Devil,
Our slick, red-tie'd politician would have you believe
   he has done NOTHING WRONG
it's always someone else's fault
   for all the guns in the world
for the deaths of the innocent
   for the ability to turn the gyres into graveyards,
lying straight-faced to your constituents.
What kind of man would allow
their wife, children, friends
to be dragged through the lurid mire,
   of a public court
like slop hogs
then,
with a shit-eating grin,
   call the country "a pile of garbage"
veterans "Suckers and Losers"
         yet promise the breasts of the Golden Calf,
   It reminds me of a joke:
there are only two moving parts
to an orange clown politician,
         the ass and the mouth,
and they're both interchangeable.

trees barked in the black light while rocks rolled on velvet rugs in the afterglow of lava lamp eruptions to expose the corruptions of shadows framed on celluloid phlegm coughed up from the coffin that hammer had nailed shut to sail the see of christopher lee burning in wicker so he might later be placed as a sticker on your tv as an ad ad libbing the fibs of rosemary's baby in a crib after it learned to crawl then draw attention to the omen of the amens of a baby man carrying the briefcase of the end times when the seasons will no longer rhyme but shortchange you a nickel and a dime in the wage theft crime of intelligent design that posits potus as a god above the laws of women and men

Regime Change

A table built of alphabet
Knocked over
Scatters across the floor

Arranging various spellings
All day long

A lettered future it ain't

History is a Muenster

Drill, Baby, Drill

At the oil
slick covered bay

Dear Leader opines:

Look at the rainbow.
It's a beautiful thing,

everyone says.
Drill, baby, drill.

Eliot Katz

One Small Reason the President's Border Wall and Muslim Ban Are Wrong

With crazy power over weaponization
and environmental regulation,
Trump is clearly a greater threat
to the planet
than the people he is trying to keep out.

Andrew K. Peterson

Reparations for a Riot Deferred

(Please, please, please)
Lugging Xmas bundles
consider snow's vibrations
the bronze coated statue
slung left, right leg strident
torqued to cast aside, to walk on by ...

what I know about ex-Boston Mayor Kevin White: the
strife of city busing exposed Boston's shining-city-on-the-
hill. A white man spears a black man with a flag pole.
Eagle-tipped. In the ragged night after Dr. King's murder,
Mayor White negotiated with The Godfather of Soul to
broadcast a Garden concert. 60 grand agreed; 15 paid in
advance, 45 still in balance to this day he struts across the
snows of Jupiter into whatever false future a Saturn blast
beholds. History. Going without haste from this
imperceptible past. A stamp on a ledger in Government
Center.

The night James Brown Saved Boston: the angry Garden
crowd ricocheted forward, took it to the stage. He
welcomed them on, then soothed them with a song:

> That's Life
> It's a Man's Man's Man's World/I Lost
> Someone/Bewildered
> Get it Together
> Please, Please, Please

Tear it all down, & rebuild
 with the hunk of The Godfather Face.
(Suggested cost: $45,000.)
Snow vibrates the sun on bronzed shoulders.
What balances these relations
in time? What reparations
for a riot, deferred?

Alex Gildzen

For the Children in the Camps

I wish
my arms were bigger
so I cd hold you
my back broader
so I cd carry you
out of yr cages
to yr parents

I wish
we cd sway together
in a hammock
while I make up
a story abt an elephant
like Dad did for me

I wish
I cd make you laugh

Doc Janning

I sing Kaddish for America
not just for we who are Jews
but for those of all faiths
all belief systems
who have dared dream the dream
in this troubled land

A dream
of love and inclusion for all
of fact over opinion and "alt-fact"
of science over denials
of equality not privilege
of love and compassion over fear
of no more bias bigotry and misogyny
of calm discussion over empty rhetoric

A dream
of "... liberty and justice for all ... "
of representatives who actually
represent the people who elect them
of no more gerrymandering
of no more bureaucrats
unqualified for their positions
of no more freely available weapons of war
on our streets
of no one going hungry
of everyone having adequate housing
and medical care
of everyone having bodily autonomy
of everyone being well-educated
and capable of critical thinking

I sing Kaddish for America
land of lost dreams
our fifty stars gone dim
our "… sweet land of liberty …"
gone sour

I sing Kaddish for America

Beau Beausoleil

Election Results

The weight of your child's fever
can bring you to your knees

While outside
the distance between ourselves
and anyone else's suffering
is lengthening

And after the last reason is examined
we will all lie down in the fever bed
 together

Luisa A. Igloria

Imminent

I read in the news that the supervolcano
in the Phlegraean Fields near Naples
is sputtering dangerously awake. It's not even
melodrama. A massive eruption would plunge
the whole world into a global winter that would mean
game over. In Dante's *Inferno*, hell is a series of nine
concentric circles descending into the bowels
of the earth. Lucifer's trapped in the deepest one:
an ice pit, no warmth, no sun. The Roman poet Virgil
is Dante's psychopomp— a kind of usher, a conductor
of souls into the afterlife. At first I thought they
entered this realm by boat, through the crater lake
of a volcano. But when I reviewed the passage,
at the start of his journey Dante is lost in a dark
wood. Then he and his guide enter the *vestibule* of hell,
before Charon picks them up in his ferry. I can appreciate
these little touches— how, even as he must have felt his
world (like ours) to be falling apart, *vestibule* conveys
a semblance of order, keeps some of the horrors at bay.
But It's also a reminder: so much evil is running around
right now, dressed in tuxedos and driving expensive
          electric
cars, preaching incivility as virtue, burning books.
No one knows what's going to happen. But even if it
          means
climbing over Satan's frozen rump and genitals with Dante
and Virgil, I want to finish the course, ascend the last
hill and come out of this doomscape, back into the light.

Sheri Reda

Tea Break Over,
Back On Yer 'Eads

Somebody
please say
they done good,

made
so much
noise the king

noticed
them. Tell
them the situation

is
no longer
perilous. Their fears

are
eating them,
and the rocks

they
hide behind
dank as ever.

Somebody
tell them
this one thing:

Whipped
into froths
of exuberance for

one
sterling moment,
they are still

just
the service,
not the served.

Alex Gildzen

The Nite the Lights Went Out at the White House

fires outside his window
so the president
cowers in a bunker
wetting his diaper

a sick nation
coughs
droplets of shame

Beau Beausoleil

New Year
In The Zones
Of Conflict

You turn
away
from the

burning
clouds
and watch
the body
of the
New Year
be buried
again

Eliot Katz

Poems and/or Anti-Poems

Will America's military leaders really go after leftist critics
of Trump, as he promised on the campaign trail? When I
    met
Nicanor Parra in New York in 1987, after Allen Ginsberg
    had
translated his St. Mark's reading and then asked Andy
    Clausen
and I to take Nicanor to a Swedish theater group's
    performance
of "Kaddish" at The Palladium club, one question I asked
    him
was how he had managed to write such strong poems
    under Pinoche's
repressive dictatorship in Chile. There was a need,
Nicanor answered, for subtlety and indirection, so that's
    where
the idea of anti-poems had come to him. Will I have to start
    writing
anti-poems at some point during these next four autocratic
Trump years? Will it be necessary to develop a new form
    of
disappearing digital literary code? With a president who
    wears
long neckties to hide a long history of criminal deeds, how
    quickly could
Trump move from targeting undocumented workers to
    late-night
comedians and then late-night writers? If gravity and anti-
    gravity

ever met in full view of the human eye, would there be
an explosion of ethical values? Could a mixing of poetry
        and anti-poetry
potentially reverse America's eye-gouging right-wing
        drift?
Until social repression hits a high-alarm shriek, I'll hold off
on writing only anti-poems and will instead keep saying
directly, at least in some of my poems, that Trump is a
        malignant
narcissist sexual predator who, judging from his
        incoherent rambling
about sharks and Hannibal Lecter, surely has good reasons
        to threaten
the U. of Pennsylvania not to release his near-failing
        college grades.

Andrew K. Peterson

Lush And Festival

June rain could make a lot of money
instead of washing these cars for free.

I didn't forget to mean
the means of production value

are controlled by Brautigan's ghost
(my device thinks I wrote *Beautician*).

Listen, ya dumb! what I mean is:
grow
& go ahead in rain
that stills the morning breeze.

what I mean is
"yea, they budded lush and festival in the dark
silence of summer agony."

what I mean is o mikron —
omega —
a declaration of peace

Flowers and opera. Lush and festival.
The grounding heart of a saudade warrior.

Carol Dorf

When I pronounce the word future
after Wislawa Szymborska

I notice what a good scrabble word it would be
using up two u's like that. Someone on Twitter
wrote she was praying the president wouldn't
start a war this weekend. I have lots of plans,
too. Conflicting political events on Saturday
and a play about the Middle East to see on Sunday.
I would really like to see Sunday. There are poems
I want to read. I need to prepare a calculus final
because my colleague and I agreed to talk about
it on Monday. Tonight M and her sons are coming
to dinner. We'll do a bit of Passover, partially
multicultural, partially because their Jewish
grandmother is dead and can't do it for them
though I think when she married a Danish man
goodbye to a musty religion was part of that.
On the other hand, I wanted my child to take
some of that history into the future. My mother-in-law
played a fierce game of scrabble and showed up
at demonstrations all of her life. I would like
to pronounce the word future with her confidence.

Beau Beausoleil

Poem For
My County

I will awaken you I said
when the severed branch
of the maple tree grows back
and sparrows once again settle
on it singing
I will not wake you to say that
children continue to be killed
in Gaza in multiples of suffering
and that I am afraid to cry
while alone next to you
You once told me to only wake you
when I saw that you were already weeping
 in your sleep
So many of us can no longer wait that long

Ronald Mars Lintz

Dumpus & Crust

The last of our democracy
slips down the drain in Moscow
as person after person is fired.
This is not governing; this
is chaos intended to tear us
apart, and it is. From parks to
education to helping those in
need--greed and ego have
run rampant, and now we,
the people, are huddling
in the cold night wondering
when to head out with our
muskets to take on a world
not even real. Dumpus, Dante
 built a home for you long ago
 in ice, and I suspect that you are
already there.

Cosimo Lamanna

The Last Bullet

They'll come to hunt us down
At the end of the feast
All of the same breed
House by house
Thought by thought
Color by color
Sickness by sickness
Hate by hate
Arrogance by arrogance

They'll come to strip the lock
From the keys we clutch so tightly
The doormat from beneath our soles
The doorbell from our fingertips

With fire still burning in the gullet
They'll throw us into a final test
And the one who spits the farthest
Will earn the honor of the last bullet.

Gerard Donnelly Smith

Inaugural

We shall not use the term maiden,
nor beginning, for one, this voyage
is not a peaceful circumnavigation
but a shake-down cruise disguised
as a love boat leaving in its wake
inescapable oxymorons.
This is not really initiatory, we
all experienced an initiation before,
hazing included, nor shall we
call this the first in a series
of events or activities, we
shall not invite any negativity
into our ball where everyone, we
hope can dance to their own tune.

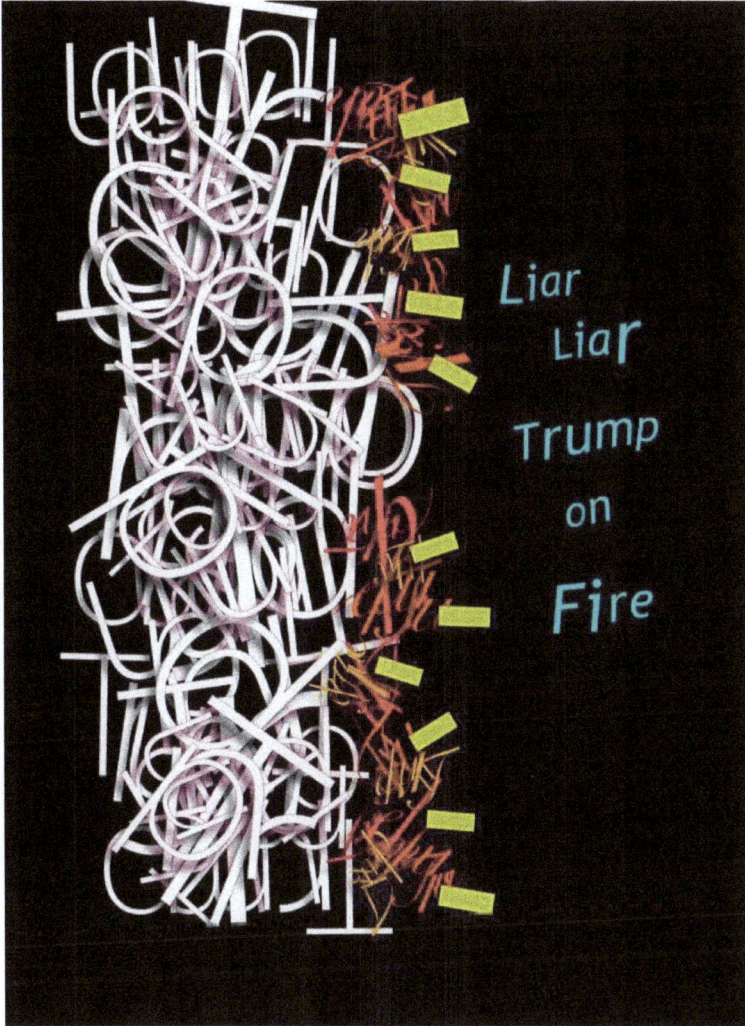

Liar
Liar
Trump
on
Fire

Mark Young

Today the post-
woman brought
me a lifesize full-
color effigy of
Donald Trump. I
put it in the back-
yard to keep the
fruit bats at bay.

The plan backfired.
So much orange
that the fruit bats—
dare I say it?—
went bananas &
have started
arriving in ever-
increasing numbers.

Today the post-
woman brought
me a red Donald
Trump cap. Slightly
different from
the ones you'll
find worn by
the man &; his
slavish devotees.

This one addressed
to those outside
the country who
may or may not
remember the Ugly
American of Graham
Greene fame but are
aware of him anyway.

MAKE AMERICA
GRATE AGAIN.

Today the post-
woman brought
me a red face
mask with a
White House decal
over the mouth
area. Inside was a
label: *hand-made*
by Ivanka Trump
from one of Our
Beloved Leader's
ties. Delicately em-
broidered around the
bottom border: *Pro-*
duct of Bangladesh.

Today the post-
woman brought me
the new collection
of short poems by
DoNuts T.®ump
entitled *Massive*
fraud has been
found.

A sample example:

> They talk about
> glitches. How many
>   glitches did they
> find? Oh, gee, we
> had a glitch, 5000
> votes. We're like a
> third-world country.

The book is
edited by Rudlie
Giulieandlieandlie
& selected copies
are signed in hair-
product by both
RuG & the DTs.

Today the post-
woman brought
me a CD of DoNuts
T.®ump trying
to recite *The Star-
Spangled Banner*
when I'd asked for
a sharp-angled
spanner to be de-
livered. *Why this?*
I asked. Listen to
the words, she said.
I just wanted to point
out to the oft-critical
poet that there's some-
one even more inept
at using the correct
words than I am, &
he used to be the
fucking President.

Today the post-
woman brought
me a punching
bag in the like-
ness of Donald
Trump. I'm

thinking about
sending it back.

a + b − a = b —
I've done the
math. If you
knock the shit

out of a shithead
you're left with
just the head. &;
who wants to
be left with a
head like that?

Alex Gildzen

After the March

on bus home
with my sign
("Poets against Hate")
everyone else
voted for the other

one screams
that we marchers
shd be flown
to Cambodia
to drown
in a river
of diaper water

I have poems
in my pocket

somehow
we'll make it

Frank Johnson

A Death Foretold

I'm writing, Don, to say how deeply struck
I've been by the quiet dignity you're showing
in the show trials you're currently undergoing.
Has anyone ever suffered such bad luck
as you have since the election which you won
was stolen by those evil Deep State people?
The accusations against you are unbelievable.
How could a modest man like you have done
half the things they say? – you, a saint,
a living, breathing US paragon
to whom the alt-right Christian God is wed.
Your Shallow-State state will trump the Deep-State
        state.
Stay strong until Novem... Oh dear! You've won.
Now satire, just like democracy, is dead.

Stasha Powell

Wise Hope

Aching world, I see you,
where wars scar the soil,
and injustice wears heavy boots.
Hope feels like a frail whisper,
trembling beneath the shadow of despair.
Why bother?
Why cradle the fragile flame
when storms howl so loudly?

Ordinary hope, they call it,
a desperate thread of desire,
clinging to what cannot be held.
But wise hope—
it is the quiet inhale before action,
the steadfast gaze into the heart of suffering,
the certainty that meaning persists,
even when outcomes dissolve
into the unknowable mist.

Wise hope does not dream of gardens
while standing in ash.
It stands in ash,
and plants seeds anyway,
trusting the rain, the soil,
the shift of seasons we cannot command.
It knows that uncertainty
is not an enemy,
but a spacious field where change grows.

Show up.
Two words carved into the temple of being.
Face the 65 million displaced souls,
the forests crumbling into sand,
the oceans rising like an unanswered question.
Show up for the bedside vigil,
the ballot box,
the breaking moment
when humanity falters,
yet finds its footing again.
Wise hope does not flee the present,

nor does it adorn it with false light.
It bows to impermanence,
to the inevitable turning
of every wheel and tide.
It breathes where apathy cannot,
moves where fear stills.
It trusts in the unseen ripples
of even the smallest act.

Moe Shapiro

A poem, inspired by nightmares before the T Rump inauguration

Humanity hurtles toward the abyss
egged on by demon-voiced desire
"Drill, baby, drill!", sucking green
goddess Mother Nature dry
Monstrously-egoed big babies
who never sucked the breast of flesh
must now have an entire planet
to suck up with fury
Never sated rapist vampires
grabbing the Earth by her pussy and
declaring "She asked for it!"
Will they shoot their docile mistresses
before their final suck, pistol in mouth
before the gasoline pyre reduces them
to ashes left behind for grim survivors
to spread upon a dying land?

Naomi Buck Palagi

We cannot be mesmerized
                    -PB

What we Do Instead

Friend,
look at me, please
hold me in your eyes, keep me
looking at you and not –

it is so easy, an involuntary twitch,
to look and be lost, it is so
close
hold me in your eyes and I, you—
together we, half-blind with not looking,
reach out to friends not yet

irrevocably frozen with fear, together we
pull all our senses, pool
all our senses and,

holding each other in our sight,
we
fight.

John Stickney

Our Lord and Pin Cushion
(Trump Found Poem)

If I took this shirt off
you would see a beautiful
beautiful person

But you would see wounds all over.
I've taken a lot of wounds
I can tell you

More than I suspect
any president
ever

(Trump quoted remarks - 06/22/2024)

John Stickney

Our Orange Lord and Pin Cushion - Part 2
(Trump Found Poem)

Some Commandments (from which I have been granted
Immunity by the current Supreme Court)

"You know,
I think that if they weren't there already,
I would've come up with those commandments.
Right?

Yeah, I think so.
Don't you?

That's something
I could've done."

(Trump quote from appearance on 06/24/2024)

Kristian Carlsson

Double Edged

1. *Fired from Media for Using VPN*

> I'd like to send a message with a shooting star —
> but all passes in a moment's flash and I lose the
> pace
> Qu Yuan, from Nine Songs (c. 300 BCE)

In China
fresh from the West
energy drink and teabag brands
chocolate and soda brands
ice cream, beer and wine
But no West End World Wide Web

In China
fresh from the West
coffee shops and fast food chains
every luxury fashion house
plain wear, street wear, sports wear
But no West End World Wide Web

In China
fresh from the West
home interior stores
convenience stores
department stores
But no West End World Wide Web

In China

fresh from the West
makeup, jewellery, perfume
cars, computers, phones
elevators, tech and toys
But no West End World Wide Web

In China
fresh from the West
cyber security and digitalization
models and commercial faces
and Mickey Mouse with a smile
But no West End World Wide Web

2. *Project Nimbus*

> Stood the house south
> or north of the bridge
> by this forsaken harvest
> Anonymous, from "Fighting South of the Castle"
> (c. 124 BCE)

In Palestine the Google weapon
technology systems are in effect
But don't affect the googling
aspect of the West

In Palestine the algorithms recognize
who's worth the cost of a missile
But don't affect the googling
aspect of the West

In Palestine the AI clouds pass on
whereabouts of targets heading home

But don't affect the googling
aspect of the West

In Palestine calculations of gain
omit deduction for collateral damage
But don't affect the googling
aspect of the West

By contract a public boycott
won't allow for breach of contract
But don't affect the googling
aspect of the West

Corporate employee protests
won't allow for breach of contract
But don't affect the googling
aspect of the West

In Palestine those drones
lure targets out in the open
by playing recorded cries
of women and infants
But don't affect the googling
aspect of the West

3. *Regained Control of the Country*

> China thinks we're a stupid country, a very stupid
> country.
> [...]
> They are developing. Well, we're a developing
> nation too.

Donald Trump, interviewed by Bloomberg News
(October 15, 2024)

USA banning George Orwell
That's taintless for running it by the book
But no West End aspect of the West
USA braving Game Over
That's flawless for running things by Musk
But no West End aspect of the West

USA behaving God Only Knows
That's dauntless for spinning things by tilt
But no West End aspect of the West
In USA bullying and name-calling
become presidential privilege
New West End prospect of the West
A continual feed superseding
paraphrases of relevance
New West End prospect of the West
The AI of USA fighting the AI of China
for shares of the fake news quota in effect
What Trump says Xi says Trump
said Xi will say Trump has said
New West End prospect of the West
On-standby granted voting rights
for fetuses will supersede convicts
in privilege for presidential elections

New West End prospect of the West
But no West End aspect of the West
Counterculture deemed domestic
terrorism makes the mainstream
vigilantly responsive to manipulations

from the White House of the White House
ending the West aspect of the West

Quotes from Chinese poets: Qu Yuan translated by
Nicholas Morrow Williams; Anonymous poet translated
by Kristian Carlsson.

Eileen R. Tabios

'NAKU

—*After Kendrick Lamar' s 2025 Super Bowl Halftime Show*

Be Proud. Stand
Up. Be
Proud.

Stand Up. Be
Alive. Stand
Up.

Be Joyous. Stand
Up. Be
Joy.

Stand up. Be
Powerful. Stand
Up.

Be Power. Stand
Up. Be
Firm.

Stand up. Be
Flexible. Stand
Up.

Be Effective. Stand
Up. Be
Achievement.

Stand Up. Be
Alive. Stand
Up.

Be Empathetic. Stand
Up. Be
Empathy.

Stand Up. Be
True. Stand
Up.

Be Truth. Stand
Up. Be
Authentic.

Stand Up. Be
Genuine. Stand
Up.

Be Darkness. Stand
Up. Be
Dark.

Stand Up. Be
Light. Stand
Up.

Be Smart. Stand
Up. Be
Knowledge.

Stand Up. Be

Alive. Stand
Up.

Be Stand-Up. Stand
Up. Be
Justice.

Stand Up. Be
Honest. Stand
Up.

Be Brave. Stand
Up. Be
Proud.

Stand up. Be
Alive. Stand
Up.

Be Self-Aware. Stand
Up. Be
Alive.

Stand Up. Be
Alive. Stand
Up.

Be Present. Stand
Up. Be
Now.

Stand Up. Be
Alive. Stand

Up.

Be Here. Stand
Up. Be
Aware.

Stand. Do not
Be Like
Them.

N.B. The poem's form is a Chained Hay(na)ku.

Doc Janning

I mourn for our country
and decry
the willful ignorance
greed
and lust for power
which brought us to this state

I mourn
for all who are or will be affected
by pronouncements
and actions
of those ill-fit

for elected office
I mourn
and I call for resistance

Resist!
in any and every legal manner

Vote!
against those who aid and abet
this assault
on our Constitutional republic

Vote!
as though your life depends on it
for it does

Vote!
though you may never have voted before

Register and Vote!
Non-voters
would have been the difference

Speak Out!
Use your voice
and voice the truth
the truth of reality

Call!
your Senators
your Congressional Representatives
your state Senators and Representatives
your local officials

Protest!
the harmful rollbacks
the unthinking uncaring edicts
the bigotry and misogyny
the unconstitutional acts
the ignorant and unqualified bureaucrats

Unite!

Stand!

Resist!
"

Ronald Mars Lintz

Together

Last time, I marched through
the streets wearing a pink
hat and chanting slogans in
song. This time, no march
will work to stop the torching.
We must come together to
stop the madness that spreads
against our very needs. Nature
stripped, medicine decried,
truth pushed away. We must
come together to remember
who we are so that we can
turn away from the fear and
hatred that is spreading. The
storm has arrived. We must
help each other and be ready
to rebuild.

Rachael Ikins

Reality Show

The president says every day is a new episode. His
unreality show. He talks to the people in his head "they
like me there" his disease has spread.

Defenders filibuster as long as their bladders hold. The
people phone in 1700 calls a minute. No matter.

He wanted a certain super hero game set for Christmas.
Intricately carved figureheads hollow as puppets. A game
even Marvel Comics will not make into a movie. The
buddy who tossed live mice into a blender to thrill his
friends, to feed the snake, is in charge of animal welfare.

We the animals. The poorest of his faithful
used for their addiction to false information, who never
investigated or researched more than their navels, other's
convictions discarded along with those in nursing homes,
hospitals, schools, no-thank-you for your service.

Soon will we all be required to speak Russian? That
autocrat celebrates the reign of the TV star. Is he connected
to the neighborhood boy who lied when someone asked
where he was from, the one who stole lunch money from
other kids' lockers , who held a hand out to daddy rather
than do the work? This man.

Is he a man or a fat raton, stalked his friends' sisters, hid in
bushes outside their windows while they undressed. Better
close your curtains, too late his pudgy fingers already riffle

your underwear drawer pawing lace and silk, holding
dirty panties' musk to his face, he breathes deep.

If we have to learn a foreign language there will be speech
impediments. They took down the education department,
fired teachers and sent air traffic controllers home. First
week, worst two plane crashes in twenty years? Blame his
Vendetta against the Past.

May have been an imperfect man the previous guy, but he
was a true leader, gone before the carnage.

******

Tables of worker bees in offices pass out Koolaid in red
solo cups where news media used to work. As far as
education they dicker words, like the definitions of 'male'
and 'female.' Play at god mandating only two sexes or is it
genders—hard to tell when the bros club consists of a
coupla men married to five or eight women with 9 idk or is
it 11 kids between 'em, who didn't know how to use birth
control. A landslide of offspring and ex wives.

Life starts at erection! It's in the Bible "let no man spill his
seed on the earth or hair will grow on his palms." How old
is that verse? Seems ignorance lasts as long as granite
on this planet.

The captain of the team pulls his special coin for tossing
from his extra long jacket pocket with a tiny hand. Brought
it to the chess match. Checkers at the door. 'Round the
world players move dictators and oligarchs. Meanwhile

Bishop takes king when she asks for simple mercy. Add her name to the s hit list.

The faithful decide it patriotic to burn the crops their livelihood depends on. Across the border. Opponents say, "don't look at me with your hand out, I'll charge you
        triple."
Friends who helped douse Los Angeles fires, treated like enemies. Is it black and white/ good guys vs. villains? Guess which role he tantrumed over when another kid got the part?

Drones worked four years, steadily writing an agenda he claims he knew nothing about. Before the previous leader stepped down, pages stacked an empty desk, a box of Sharpies resolute waiting for Savior to do what he is told by the raton, the chess champions .

He doesn't read books "because who has time," vendetta show sells "Bibles and gold sneakers, get a matched set!" Compile lists, all people who speak truth to power. The Emperor struts naked down the street resplendent in rouge. "Let them eat cake!"

*****

A waitress who smells of Jasmine brings beer to our table. Asks what my teeshirt says. I stretch it so she can see Ruth Bader Ginsburg's fierce face. "Women belong in all places decisions are being made." She wraps her arms around her body, joy reading this.

Suddenly we three #resistance fighters, #community in a
sports bar where the 20 TVS show football and women's
basketball, no episodes of the game show horror we live in.

For now.

Ruth said our national mascot should not be the bald eagle
but a pendulum. She tried to outlive death to protect the
country and laws she'd devoted a life's work to, Davy
Crockett as the bright lights masking darkness barreled
down the horizon. Who works out at the gym with
pancreatic cancer? A hero.

She is right, what goes around comes around. FAFO. It's a
law you can't bend,
pretend mr prez.
It takes us all in the end.

I hope I live to see the pendulum knock
you into the blender,
where you threw little kids and students, and single moms
with triple jobs, brown skinned people, queer folk and a
planet,

when your buddy, the gravel-voiced worm presses
"smoothie."

Garin Cycholl, Kirk Robinson,
and William Allegrezza

Trumpus 2116: The last poem-novel of the 21st Century

I am an expert negotiator
I am a truth-speaker
I am a railroads man

I am a dove for war
I am a tomahawk for peace
I am a New Jersey taxpayer
I am an award-winning developer
I am a smoker of expensive weeds
I am prize-winning writer of jokes and memoir
I am a driver of half-tracks, bulldozers, and pay-loaders
I am an endless lover
I am a water-gater

I am a teapot-domer
I am not my opponent
I am a TV crawler loaded with unbroken quotation
I am a speak-truther
I am a phone on speed dial for Mike Pence
I am at a loss for words

I am the unhinged memory of your father
I am your last option

www.ingramcontent.com/pod-product-compliance
Lightning Source LLC
Chambersburg PA
CBHW072352090426
42741CB00012B/3016